# On the run

Dan has a bucket of
oats for Gus, the goat.

Dan and Nat hop in Mum's van to go to the shops. Gus thinks he can go, too. He trots to the road.

Gus jogs up the road
and sees a truck with
a load of foam.

Gus roams up the road.
He stops next to a big oak
tree and munches on weeds.

A green toad croaks at Gus.

The toad hops off.
Gus trots along with him.

They get to the pond and
the toad jumps in. Gus sees
a boat and jumps into it.

The boat floats on the
pond. But then it tips up.
Splash! Gus is soaking wet.

Gus sinks into the mud. The thick, wet mud sticks to him.

He gets up and runs back
to the road. He is a mess.

The truck tips the load
of foam on to the road.
Gus runs into it.

The foam sticks to Gus.

Just then, Mum's van
stops next to Gus.

"Quick!" Nat yells. "We
need to grab this sheep.
It is on the run."

Dan sees that it is not
a sheep. "It is just Gus!
**He** has been on the run!"

# Words to blend

| | | |
|---|---|---|
| bucket | van | shops |
| thinks | jogs | sees |
| truck | next | munches |
| weeds | green | off |
| along | jumps | wet |
| thick | sticks | back |

# Before reading

**Synopsis:** Gus, the goat, heads off after the van. On the way he falls in a pond, mud and a load of foam. He looks like a sheep after these mishaps.

**Review phoneme/s:** th/th ch ng sh ai ee igh

**New phoneme:** oa

**Story discussion:** Look at the cover, and read the title together. Ask: *Who do you think the main character of this story will be? What kinds of things might happen?*

**Link to prior learning:** Display the grapheme oa. Say: *These two letters are a digraph, they make one sound together. They make the /oa/ sound, as in* boat. *This digraph usually comes in the middle of a word.* How quickly can children find and read three oa words on page 12? (load, foam, road)

**Vocabulary check:** Roam – walk around freely without being stopped. Turn to page 5 and read the sentence, *Gus roams up the road,* together. Can children think of another word that could be used instead of *roams*? (e.g. wanders)

**Decoding practice:** Give children a card with the digraph oa and letter cards or magnetic letters b, t, g, d, r. How many real words can they make? (e.g. boat, toad, goat, road)

**Tricky word practice:** Display the words *to* and *too*. Ask children to circle the tricky parts of these words. What sound do they make? (o and oo both make a long /oo/ sound.) Encourage children to look out for these tricky words in their reading.

# After reading

**Apply learning:** Can children recap the main events of the story in their own words? Ask: *Which bit do you think was funniest?*

## Comprehension

- What does Dan give Gus to eat?
- Why does Gus go out on to the road?
- Why does Nat mistake Gus for a sheep?

## Fluency

- Pick a page that most of the group read quite easily. Ask them to reread it with pace and expression. Model how to do this if necessary.

- Turn to page 4. Encourage children to read this longer sentence as fluently as possible, with appropriate pace so that the meaning is clear.

- Practise reading the words on page 17.

# Tricky words review

| | | |
|---|---|---|
| the | of | for |
| to | go | have |
| too | they | into |
| we | you | out |
| all | are | was |